MW01228631

DON'T LOSE YOURSELF

YOURSELF

A FIRST RESPONDER'S
MENTAL HEALTH PLAYBOOK

Written By: The Salty Paramedic

FOREWORD

Mental health amongst first responders is a hidden enemy that is slowly being recognized by more and more people in the field. It has plagued our professions for generations and has hung over even the strongest men and women like a dark cloud. Despite how dreary this all sounds I honestly believe we are on the right track to successfully mitigate this problem. Steps are being taken. Emotions are being analyzed. But there is still a lot of work to do.

I have spent my life surrounded by first responders and eventually became one myself. I have witnessed firsthand the traumas that we face daily and how easily they can affect families, relationships and the

3

career itself. There is a reason divorce lawyers rejoice at the mention of firefighters or police officers heading to their office.

The idea for this book has been dwelling inside my mind for years. Let's get one thing straight right off the bat: this book will not solve all your problems. I am simply using this big, compacted stack of paper to detail my experiences in successfully keeping my mental health in check (for the most part). This text is what I will refer to as "The First Responder's Mental Health Playbook," which is hilarious because I am the last guy you want to talk to about plays used in sports. Each chapter will highlight different "plays" or actions I think will help your mental psyche either instantly or over a span of time.

You might already apply some of this advice in your life. If so, that's great, and I hope it's working well for you so far! If all this is new to you, and you are currently struggling, I hope this can truly make a difference. If I've helped one person by the end of this book it has served its purpose. Above all,

Don't Lose Yourself.

CHAPTER ONE

IDENTIFY

I am convinced if there was an OB doctor and labor hall nurses at the firehouse I would have been born there. My father was a career firefighter throughout most of my life so naturally I was always at the fire station. I remember my dad being gone a lot (every third day for 24 hours at the firehouse) but he also held down multiple part time jobs as most firefighters do. Despite these long absences my mom would always take me and my sister to the station to visit him.

From an incredibly early age I was always obsessed with the trucks, flashing lights and sirens (I was oblivious to the much-dreaded lift assist that was a common occurrence). Each day I got to hang out with my dad and the guys on his crew I would slowly start to notice social cues the more I got older. One of the guys would lose their shit on another, one would choose to be silent and secluded a particular day, and in even more extreme cases there would be a complete station standoff. Grown ass men each thinking they are right and refusing to budge to hear out the other one.

These experiences I saw occurred because of things happening on a much deeper level. Behind closed doors, a first responders' social experiences while not on duty can either slowly trickle into their work life or break the dam that is holding up their mental wellbeing with a torrential flood. These can be several things: relationship trouble with your significant other, family disputes, financial issues, burnout or just a slip in judgement.

My father more than likely dealt with a lot of these, but I would never have known that growing up. Like most first responders he was a master of hiding his emotions and "staying strong" for his family. Because of this huge wall he built around himself (just like many others in our profession) I always looked at him like he was Superman. Always strong. Never showed fear. No emotion.

Now don't get me wrong, I still look at my dad as Superman (even though he is 6 inches shorter than me now). I can attribute most of my traits as a man to him and the lessons he taught me growing up. I was blessed to have a role model that was in public service to help steer me down the right path.

I think he was able to exemplify my first "play" within his life quickly: Identify. Before you try to implement any of these chapters into your life, I believe you must "identify" who you are as a person. Nothing you do from here on out is worth it if you are trying to be someone you're not. You must understand how you operate. What are your strengths and weaknesses? What made you want to get into public service? What separates you from everyone else?

My father grew up on a dairy farm (right next to Colonel Sanders if you can believe it). From an early age he was instilled with an arduous work ethic and a desire to provide for his family and help others. He would always tell me stories of how he was woken up by his mom around 4 in the morning to go help milk the cows before school. He was a ten-year-old that was learning fast what it meant to be in the workforce.

Fast forward to the age of 16 and he was still working on the farm every day while trying to navigate hanging out with friends, schooling, and trying to stay out of trouble. One day during the school year he was picked up by the sheriff and alerted there had been a terrible accident. My grandmother had fallen into a silage auger and had gotten her leg cut off.

He has not ever gone into much detail about what happened that day and what he was feeling. I can imagine knowing your mother was in a traumatic accident such as that would send you into a state of hysteria, especially because of how close they always were.

He has told me countless times when he did get there the fire department/EMS response was large and well-coordinated. He was amazed at the job they did in this high stress environment. How well they were able to keep a level head while tending to my grandmother who was in dire need of medical attention. I am happy to report my grandmother was rescued and continued to live with a prosthetic leg. I am convinced if she was never in the accident, she could have been a firefighter, cop, medic, anything she wanted to be. She was the strongest woman I had ever known. Until passing away a few years ago she was able to function better than most people with both legs intact and was able to keep a steady supply of humor and happiness for everyone she was around.

The fire chief on the scene saw a sixteen-year-old kid that needed to be steered in the right direction. My dad said this chief took him under his wing shortly after this incident and let him hang out around the firehouse. My dad fell in love with the profession quickly. The chief recognized this eagerness and was able to institute an explorer program so my dad was able to start training and go on runs with the department.

This explorer program eventually led to him volunteering at the age of 18 and learning more about the job. He got married to my mother at the age of 19 and had his first kid (me) the following year. Now what did this extremely young guy with an infant and wife do? He worked his ass off. My mother and my father worked long days and nights to support their newly made family. He had known struggle throughout his childhood. He had experienced pain and loss. But he did not let it define him.

My father **identified** who he was as a person early on. He was a farmer's son that had a strong work ethic and a wild sense of humor. His shortcoming was his temper, and he knew it. If someone pissed him off, they would know quickly and in a hurry. But he embraced this and didn't try to be someone he was not.

This temper would sometimes get him in a bad spot. He would often tell me about fights in grade school triggered by anger or his smart mouth. This carried on into his adult life where he would have verbal confrontations with coworkers he didn't see eye to eye with. But despite all the trouble this would get him in, he recognized this and was always quick to forgive. He was constantly (and still is to this day) on the path to become a better man.

The identity of a first responder is often as much of a mystery to the person themselves as to those around them. They spend so much time in their life trying to fix the problems of others around them that they don't take a second to stop and look at themselves. Often the people that are blind to who they are as a person will let it get them into trouble. This trouble can range from anything as simple as getting into a verbal altercation with your wife to suicide.

I don't want to sound bleak. I really don't. But suicide in first responders is a huge problem currently and it needs to be addressed. We need to learn to take care of ourselves just as much as we take care of total strangers lying in a totaled car on the side of a highway.

My dad identified his good attributes too, however. He knew how hard of a worker he was. After a few years of volunteering at his department he applied to be a full-time career firefighter. He did the gamut: written, physical test and interview. He was able to come out of all that with a job offer and a ticket to a career doing what he had been accustomed to love.

He spent the next twenty years as a career firefighter putting that work ethic to use: classes, new certifications and promotions. He managed a deer processing business in the winter, worked at a car wash year-round, worked EMS part time, taught HAZMAT across the state and probably a bunch of other things that I wasn't even privy to. He did all this not just to support his family but show his son just how well you can maintain good mental health while you're carrying the weight of the world on your shoulders.

My dad is retired from the fire department after a long and successful career now. He had over twenty years of traumatic calls, physically strenuous fires and unbelievable sleep schedules. He came out of it though even stronger. This is because I think my dad lived by my playbook that I'm writing right now. He essentially created this guide by his actions, and I am just the kid that was lucky enough to shadow a role model and write it all down.

Before you do anything, **identify** who you are. Are you someone that needs that family unit around you to successfully function as a first responder? Are you someone that just needs a couple good friends and hobbies to lead you through this crazy career? It doesn't matter who you are because we can all be successful in this line of work. You know who you are, you just have to find it.

I challenge you on the next page to identify who you are as a person. Summarize the type of person you truly are.

_____
_____
_____
_____
_____
_____
_____
_____
_____
_____
_____
_____
_____
_____
_____
_____
_____
_____
_____
_____
_____
_____

CHAPTER TWO

FIND YOUR WHY

My career path was similar to my father's except for the fact I did not grow up on a dairy farm. I'm sure at the age my dad was milking cows I was playing video games and begging my mom for candy at the local video rental store.

Funny enough, my dad helped create an explorers program like that fire chief had done for him so many years ago. At the age of fifteen I was able to start taking part in training, attend public education events and everything else that came with being a firefighter (anything that did not put me directly in danger because I was underage).

As this chapter is titled, I strongly believe something one must do when working in our field is to **find your why**. It can be the widely used and generic answer of "I want to help people," but I believe it is much deeper than that when you start to dissect your why.

As a kid my "why" was as simple as they come: because I want to drive the truck with the flashing lights and do badass stuff. Little did I know as I grew older and gained more life experiences my why would change quicker and more often than the sheets on a transfer ambulance's stretcher.

I was a shy kid. I would coast through elementary school with a set group of friends that I mainly acquired from my time in organized sports and boy scouts. I steered clear of any trouble and was pretty much the exact opposite of my dad growing up. He was no stranger to detention, and I trembled at the mere mention of the word.

When I reached fifteen, I got my first part-time job and started the explorers program at the same time. I finally was starting to understand what "work" meant, or at least what work was for a fifteen-year-old. I always looked forward to the weekly trainings at the firehouse, but made sure I didn't slack with my responsibilities as a high school student and part time employee at my local fast-food restaurant.

I hung out at the firehouse all through high school, even more so during my senior year when I co-oped there and spent half the day. After years of all the firehouse banter, training and runs I knew beyond a shadow of a doubt that was what I wanted to do for the rest of my life. Well, until retirement.

At the age of 18 I had officially moved up in the department from an explorer to a volunteer. Over the course of three years I had seen dead bodies, went to a few fires (Though I wasn't able to go anywhere near it) and had been to a few crazy MVAs.

My "why" had started to slowly develop into a more detailed thought. Of course, I still wanted to do it for the big red trucks, the exhilarating feeling of having the gas pedal floored at 3 am and forcing your way through doors with tools almost as big as you are. I started to realize my "why" was more for the impact I could have on other people's lives instead of my own. I started off wanting to just do this for the adrenaline side of it. I liked the feeling I got when I got to do something related to the job. It made me feel incredible.

The more runs I went on and the more complete strangers I encountered in their most vulnerable state I started to realize I didn't want to do this for just me anymore. My "why" had transformed from self-fulfilling to people pleasing. I had started to see just how much of an impact you can have on others' lives as a first responder. We could be called to someone's house at any point (day or night) and their life or family member's life could be completely decided by what we choose to do next. It's an unbelievable burden and feeling that I don't think anyone can properly translate it into words.

In my short stint as a volunteer firefighter, I had been able to witness just how many lives myself and other members of my department were able to change. I quickly discovered that as a first responder it was very common for you to have to go from a calm individual sitting at the station eating a bowl of cereal and watching trashy tv to being in the middle of an intersection with vehicle wreckage and splatters of blood around you. This change in your day could happen within minutes. And we are supposed to be able to mentally process this and continue to function as a first responder, family member and friend.

These experiences didn't deter me. Quite the opposite. I was more certain than ever that this is what I wanted to do. So, I ended my summer of volunteer firefighting and went straight to college. I signed up to get a 4-year degree in Fire Protection & Administration. A piece of paper that I was told I needed if I ever wanted to move up high in the department (I didn't think I would want to be a Chief at the time and those feelings have not changed as I sit here writing this today). I wanted the education and training, however. I was always someone that was self-motivated. Someone that wanted to be successful even as just a firefighter employed in a department in the middle of nowhere. I knew what I wanted to be since I was little and that wasn't going to change.

Four years seemed to be like an eternity at the time I was a student at my college, but now when I look back at it, I'm only able to remember a few moments of it. My first year there didn't take long for me to almost ruin my chances of getting that bachelors degree I coveted so much at the time. I was a young man, completely on my own in a small dorm room packed with ramen noodles and textbooks I didn't read as much as I should have. My parents weren't with me anymore to make sure I did the work I was supposed to or even went to class at all. This freedom I had was invigorating but ended up being more humbling than anything I had experienced in my life.

In the beginning of my first semester, I didn't do too bad. I attended my classes and worked full time at a restaurant as a cook. However, after a few months I started to accept more invites to parties and social gatherings than I should of. I would get off work at 1am, stay out until 4am and then would have to physically pull myself out of bed for class at the sound of my obnoxious alarm at 8am. As you can probably surmise, it didn't take me too long to start hammering the snooze button on my phone until I woke up hours later.

I ended up failing classes due to lack of attendance, homework not being completed and my tests being under the minimum passing grade. The mixture of all this put me under an embarrassing category called "academic probation." I was already at risk of being kicked out of school and I hadn't even been there a whole year. Shit was looking pretty bleak right? Don't worry, I found a way to make it even worse.

Turns out academic probation wasn't the only "probation" I could be put on. One night I thought it was a smart idea to drink with a bunch of my friends in my dorm (including my Resident Advisor). Someone ended up spilling the beans to the lady in charge of the building and we ended up in some head honcho's office a few days later. The zero-tolerance alcohol policy was explained to me, and I was placed on social probation as well.

So here I was not even in a year into college, and I was put on two lists that were making my future look farther and farther away. I was beaten down and didn't think it would get any better. For some reason I lost a lot of my drive I had in high school. My dad had a coming to Jesus meeting with me at the end of that school year. To summarize it, he told me I better get my shit together or my college experience was going to be over in the blink of an eye.

That summer in between my freshman and sophomore year of college I had to do a lot of soul searching. I got a job delivering pizza and spent every day doing that. It was a lot different than being in school and skipping class, I'll tell you that. It felt like a huge knot was in my stomach for those three months. If I didn't go back to school with a new mindset and proved to be responsible, I was done.

August finally came around and I found myself moving into a new dorm. I was ready to prove myself, but I was still more nervous than I had ever been. I had signed up for even harder classes that school year, and I also was taking a math class for the second time after failing it my first year.

I still remember moving in day like it was yesterday. My parents came to help me unload everything (I don't know why I had so much stuff) even though the room was smaller than a prison bathroom. As I walked in, I was greeted by a resident advisor to check in. She was beautiful, to put it simply. Long black hair, tall and a smile that made me start stuttering like I was in EMT class doing patient scenarios.

She asked me my name, and I quickly blurted it out. She then informed me I was going to be on her floor and she was my resident advisor. This dorm had co-ed floors? I had no idea. This was not going to help my case of staying ahead in my schoolwork at all. My dad had followed me into the elevator after this interaction and looked over at me and gave me a grin. I shouted out matter-of-factly to him, "I'm going to date that girl." He laughed, and we proceeded to finish moving everything in.

For once, in my life I was right. A few weeks had passed, and my roommate and I had our door open playing video games (I was still making great decisions, I know). My resident advisor was walking by and stopped in to see what we were playing. Being the smooth guy I always was, I left my computer open next to her with my social media profile pulled up. She already knew my name, but I was convinced if she sent me a friend request then the claim I had made to my dad a few weeks prior would come into fruition.

Ten minutes after she exited my room, I received a notification on my phone that my resident advisor, Brooke, had sent me a friend request. That was the happiest I had been since I left for college the year prior. After a few weeks of hanging out we had started to date (just like I told my dad). Only 8 months later I asked her to marry me, because I was more certain about that than I had ever been of anything else in my life. Thankfully, she said yes, and we got married in the summer of 2013 and finished college together. She made sure I got my shit together too; I quickly turned it all around making my way onto the dean's list and off probation.

Our life thus far has gone by like a whirlwind. I blinked my eyes and now we've had three kids together and my heart is fuller than I ever imagined it would be. I got employed in my dream job at the age of 24, with a newborn in tow. And just like, the "why" that I thought I had found back at the tender age of 18 had transformed into something totally different.

My "why" has molded itself into a few things now. First and foremost, I go to work in this career every day because of my wife and children. Now I can fully grasp why my dad worked as hard as he did when I was growing up. Not only was he providing for his family, but he did it while showcasing how to be a role model in one of the most stressful career fields. Some people might say it's a given that you would go to your job every day for your family, but you must really analyze it to fully understand.

I want my sons and my daughter to have the same type of father that I was lucky enough to have. They are getting old enough to realize now exactly how long I am gone to work at a time (24- and 48-hour shifts sometimes even longer). I want them to have the same type of present father they would have if I was at home 365 days of the year.

I'm not going to sugarcoat this. There is zero reason whatsoever you should be a deadbeat parent. You are responsible for giving your children the best life possible and just because you had a rough shift is no reason to take it out on your family. That is why "finding your why" is so crucial. In those moments of stressful thinking (traumatic runs, pediatric runs, financial troubles, etc.) you must be able to ground your mental state by being able to think about why you do it all in the first place. Does your wife make you happy? Your children? Hell, it might even be your pet cat. Anytime at work or at home I should be able to close my eyes during a stressful event and picture those things I hold dear. That image alone should be able to calm myself down enough to realize no matter how bad things may seem, I have something wholesome, absolute and real not too far away.

My family isn't the only reason I do it though. I don't go into burning buildings and sacrifice my life for my family. That wouldn't make much sense, would it? One of my big whys is seeing the change that a small person like me can make in a random stranger's life. 80-year-old granny fell down, and needs lifted back into bed? I did that. Random man went into cardiac arrest, so my crew and I jumpstarted his heart into working again. Every single day in this job is something different, and I love it. If we choose to make a difference, the change we can make in the world is tenfold.

I also would be lying if I told you I still didn't hold onto wanting that adrenaline dump I did at the age of 18. I like to do crazy shit that the public doesn't get to do. And I'm sure most of the people in our career would tell you the same. It's not shameful to want to satisfy those urges to do dangerous things, but it's up to you to train and educate yourself every chance you get to make sure you keep your coworkers and yourself safe. But that's another lecture for another book, maybe.

Challenge yourself on the next page to write down why you do it. Make sure to always look back at your reasons when you need a reminder.

Don't Lose Yourself

_____

_____

_____

_____

_____

_____

_____

_____

_____

_____

_____

_____

_____

_____

_____

_____

_____

_____

_____

_____

_____

CHAPTER THREE

RESET

If you've worked an entire career in public service and not lost yourself along the way at some point, I'd say you're lying. I always took pride in the fact that I was able to contain everything inside that I experienced on and off the job. I showed zero emotion to those around me and wore it like a badge of honor.

Just in the last 17 years alone, I've seen our career field shift into a more positive approach in sharing your feelings instead of keeping everything bottled up. Multiple agencies have taken proactive approaches like having a designated chaplain at your department to make phone calls after coworkers have been involved in a traumatic run. Sometimes just having someone else make that initial contact can have you open up and discuss how you truly feel. That one action could be all the difference in the world. I've also seen many departments conduct stress debriefings. Within a week of the event happening, they will have every unit involved with the run sit down and talk through it. I've been to many of these, and I have not seen one negative aspect to them. They bring people out of their shell, and they will discuss what they saw and did during the incident. Even though the patient outcome wasn't always positive, talking through it with your coworkers can sometimes get rid of the feeling that "you didn't do enough." Because truthfully, we all do everything in our power for a great outcome. But that's not always possible, and we need to realize that.

Throughout my time as a firefighter/paramedic I've seen some wild shit, to put it bluntly. Growing up my dad would always tell me a few stories here and there, but nothing insane. I've seen people dismembered, burned alive and decomposed beyond recognition. When you start experiencing these runs and you go about your day like nothing is wrong, you start to question if you really have lost yourself. It's not uncommon to see someone deceased and then go grab a double cheeseburger to eat five minutes later. That doesn't make us not human though, we all just process these experiences differently and find ways to cope.

It wasn't until a few years ago when I reached a breaking point. I mean this run really had me questioning my career. I didn't know how to process it, forget about it and continue to function. It really surprised me and took me off guard because I thought nothing would beat me down in this job. I was completely wrong.

It was a normal day at the firehouse. A few runs here and there. Nothing major. And then it got dispatched, 3-month-old not breathing. CPR in progress. I had gone over a decade without experiencing a pediatric cardiac arrest, and I still am beyond thankful for that. Everyone has a type of run that breaks them down, and I had just found mine.

We took out of the station like a bat out of Hell. My heart was beating out of my chest. We're always taught to stay calm. "It's not your emergency." I was screaming inside, and I didn't know if I was going to be able to quell it. I was with a paramedic ride student at the time so if there was a time to be calm and methodical in our treatment, it was now.

In what seemed like just a few minutes, we pulled up on scene. Flashing lights illuminated the front yard from cop cars, county fire units and now our med unit. We barely got out of the ambulance before a LEO shoved an unresponsive infant into our arms. I felt like I was shaking like a damn shiatsu massage chair. I was ultimately in charge of the scene, and I felt helpless.

Now we were in the back of the ambulance, and someone was driving us seconds later. I have no idea who, all I remember is saying to get us to the hospital as quickly as possible. There were four of us back there doing everything in our power for this child. We didn't know the circumstances of why he was unresponsive, and we didn't care at this point. We just wanted him back.

Compressions, ventilations, IV/IO access, medications. We did as much as we could during the short ride to the hospital, and we did it efficiently. But it didn't matter how perfect it went; a bad outcome would plague my mind for months. When we got to the hospital we transferred the patient over to the ER staff, still pulseless and not breathing.

The ER staff took over where we left off and did everything they could. Ultimately, the child did not make it. I was devastated. At the time of this run, I had two children myself at home. The whole time I was responsible for this infant, I looked down and saw them. My children mean the world to me, and here I was responsible for someone else's world. What use was all my schooling and training if I couldn't bring them back? I had unrealistic expectations due to the situation, but I couldn't see that clearly.

We cleared the hospital and went back to the station. Just like any other run. But this one was different. I wouldn't be able to sleep that night. Not due to a multitude of EMS calls. It was because every time I closed my damn eyes, I saw what I did in the back of the ambulance hours before.

I went home the following morning tired and beaten down emotionally and mentally. I didn't

want to talk about it with my wife, or anybody for
that matter. But I knew I needed to because I had
never felt this way before. I think I slept most of
that day because every second I was awake I was
thinking of the baby. I told my wife I had a bad run
and just needed a little bit of time to refocus and
regain myself.

The extra sleep didn't help at all. I finally started to
talk to my wife about the events that transpired the
night prior. I cried. I broke the fuck down. She just
listened to me, and that's what I needed at the time.
I cannot stress enough during these times of your
career; you must find someone to talk to. It could
be your significant other, a parent, a sibling, a
coworker or a friend. Talking about it once isn't
going to completely fix you, trust me. But having
that outlet is a crucial step in mending you and
getting you back to your normal self.

After my two days off I was terrified to go back to work. The chances I would experience the same type of run was astronomically low but that didn't help ease my fear. Reluctantly, I showed up and prepared myself for another 24-hour shift on the ambulance. My department had prepared a debriefing session that day with all agencies involved (the first one I had experienced). I had no idea what to expect, but I was open to doing anything that would help me not feel this way.

We showed up, and everyone was there: EMS, Fire, and Sheriff's Dept. Department heads opened the session by asking members involved to discuss what they saw and what they did during the incident. Inside my head I thought that bringing up these memories would do more harm than good. But luckily, as I was talking, I started to feel better. Just a little.

I discussed what I saw: lifeless infant handed to us, treatments performed in the back of the ambulance and then handing the infant over to the care of the hospital. I didn't talk about how it made me feel, just what happened. Other agencies spoke about their experiences. A big effort was made by the admin staff to explain that despite our best efforts, the outcome sometimes cannot be avoided. I get that, but at the time I was still in a bad space. The session concluded and everyone went about their day.

The rest of the day at work I felt a little better, but I was still a long way gone and I knew it. I didn't know what needed to happen to make me whole again, but I hoped I would figure it out soon. Weeks went by, and I was still in the same purgatory. It was starting to affect my work and home life. I felt burnout at work all the time, every time dispatch sent us somewhere I was triggered. I didn't want to be there. I didn't want to do this job anymore.

At home I had become my worst enemy. I wasn't a present father or husband. You can only blame your work experiences so much on your attitude before you start to realize you're the problem. As a first responder, we're dealt a shit hand. We are put into situations that can fracture our mental well-being and then we're supposed to put the pieces back together and continue to function. For you reading this right now, no matter how broken you are, I promise you can be put back together. You just must use the proper tools.

This brings me to my third play: **reset.** You might just need to do this once in your career. Or 50 times. There's no limit to maintaining your mental well-being. After weeks of being stuck in this rut, I knew I needed to do something quick. So, I took a vacation. Not an island getaway (that would have been nice, but we work in EMS remember). I stayed home for a week with my wife and children. We went out and had little fun experiences around town, but you know where I wasn't? At work.

I was doing a complete mental reset. I knew my family grounded me, so I took a week off to be with them and not with the job. You might be single with no kids and have experienced the same mentally devastating situation. You know what you need to do? Take vacation or use sick time. Yes, sick time. Anyone that says mental wellbeing isn't important enough to call in sick is part of the damn problem. Take a break and reset your mental psyche. Go out and do what makes you happy, makes you forget for the time being.

I'd be lying if I said you're never going to remember these traumatic events after you reset. But you will get better and eventually become whole again. Time is sometimes the best medicine. As months and years go by, you gain new memories and slowly start to not remember as much about the old ones.

Don't Lose Yourself

Reset yourself, you can't stay broken forever. Everyone around you depends on you, you've got this.

Write down the worst type of call you have experienced or could experience on the following page (only if you want to). Then promise yourself you will take time to properly perform a mental reset if you need to.

CHAPTER FOUR

SHOW COMPASSION

You would think an individual that signed up to help people for a living would have compassion dripping from every pore in their body, correct? That's not always the case. I believe I have witnessed every type of personality during my career already, and the more toxic ones can transfer over to your coworkers like a plague.

Frequent flyer is a term that is now universally recognized even among the public. You've got an individual that chooses to call 911 on a consistent basis (sometimes multiple times a day), whether it be for a "legitimate" reason or not. A lot of times you will find crews running on this individual in the middle of the night for a tummy ache after just leaving the hospital hours before. Compassion is sometimes hard to be found in this type of situation, because you as a first responder cannot mentally comprehend why someone would "waste" resources for something you wouldn't call 911 for yourself. I get it, I really do. This whole chapter's "play" is something I probably struggle with more than anything else. They don't call me The Salty Paramedic for nothing.

Throughout my life I have met hundreds of frequent flyers. Some hilarious, some dickheads and some that just make you sad. I can recall many times getting woken up in the middle of the night by someone calling for the fifth shift in a row for the same complaint. I was probably cursing a lot under my breath, and I would venture to say I was not showing them the same compassion that I would another patient.

But you know who else was a frequent flyer? My late grandfather. For years he was in terrible health:

diabetic, obese and falling frequently. He was my father's dad, and one of the people responsible for teaching my dad hard work ethic on that dairy farm he grew up on many years ago. My grandfather was a farmer most of his life and then worked in a factory every day up until his retirement. After retiring, himself and my granny would watch my sister and I at their house every day while my parents went to work. You didn't hear any bitching from him, you helped family out. Bottom line.

He was always supportive of the line of work my dad and I were in. He loved the fire department and always talked to the guys every chance he got. When his health started to decline, and he started to fall a lot I remember my dad and I going over there to try and help him up off the floor. In the beginning, when he had some strength himself, we were able to successfully do it by ourselves. But after getting diagnosed with cancer, it took us calling 911 for more manpower each time he fell. My dad and I hated doing it, because that's what we did for a living. Nobody wanted to go on a lift assist.

But one time that we called 911 stuck out to me more than any other. The EMS crew that showed up had a paramedic that had been doing the job longer than I had been alive. I mean this politely when I say it, he was almost as old as my grandfather was himself. Nobody ever had anything bad to say about this paramedic. He had been doing the job for decades and still treated it like it was his first year (I even had the pleasure of riding with him during some of my ride time in EMT school). This time was late during the night, most certainly after this crew had already gone to bed. They walked inside the house like they were seeing him for the first time (it most certainly wasn't) and were extremely professional and had friendly banter back and forth with my grandfather before helping us pick him up.

My whole perspective changed at this point. I had already been working EMS a few years at this time, and just like any other new guy I thought I already had the job figured out. I thought it was completely excusable to act like a burnt-out douchebag because you've had to run your dick off for years. But here was this paramedic, doing the job longer than anyone I've ever met. He was riding the box and making calls on frequent flyers with a smile on his face and better patient care than a brand-new guy.

That paramedic didn't know anything about how my grandfather had gotten to this position. He could have assumed that he had been a piece of shit his entire life and had been abusing the 911 system. My grandfather was one of the hardest working men I knew and had been dealt a bad hand in the later stages of his life. He was embarrassed when we had to call 911 for him, but this paramedic had made him feel like nothing was wrong and to not be ashamed.

So now each day I work I make a conscious effort to be less judgmental and more **compassionate**. When I harbored hateful feelings for having to get up in the middle of the night for the same patient weeks on end, I was only hurting myself. It's hard to stay positive in a world of negativity.

I have seen many providers that have built themselves on a piss poor attitude and fake smiles while on scenes. How you treat your patients will only carry over into how you act in your personal life. If you cannot treat your patients compassionately, how are you ever going to take care of yourself?

So, my challenge to you: treat every patient like it's your first time seeing them. You don't know how they got to their current state. What they've gone through as a person. It's not our job to judge someone, but to offer a hand. To be that light that they needed when they called 911. Be a better provider and in turn be a better person.

Challenge yourself to write about a time you were upset about a frequent caller on the next page. Then showcase ways you can show compassion and improve patient care as a first responder.

The Salty Paramedic

_____

_____

_____

_____

_____

_____

_____

_____

_____

_____

_____

_____

_____

_____

_____

_____

_____

_____

_____

_____

_____

_____

CHAPTER FIVE

INVEST IN YOURSELF

Self confidence is something I've always struggled with. I was a shy and chubby kid that hated looking at myself in the mirror. I had some friends, but you would never see me talking and initiating conversations with a new group of people I wasn't familiar with. I was never the type of kid that would want to challenge myself by doing something that didn't come easy. Unfortunately, these traits carried over into the early years of my career.

As I discussed earlier in the book, I always knew that my end game was to be a firefighter. That's what I wanted to do without a shadow of a doubt. But something I've discovered recently was being stagnant was proving detrimental to my mental health.

When I initially got hired to my full-time department, my first year of employment kept me busier than I had ever been in my life. I was immediately put into a three-month EMT class to get my certification, while also going through a fire academy at the same time to get all my training hours that were needed to get my state fire certification. One month after obtaining my EMT certification I was approached by my department to see if I was interested in attending a paramedic class. Be a paramedic? I never had a dream of that. I remember seeing medics back home starting IVs while on a call and me saying in my mind, "I will never do that."

But getting asked this question in the middle of this tsunami of certifications and work I was in the process of completing was the perfect timing in my opinion. I was motivated. I was accomplishing a bunch of things at once and I only wanted to do more. It felt good. Really good. It was a tremendous workload, but I was more focused than ever. I truly believe the more stress you are put under transforms you as a person. You can start to handle more. When problems are presented to you, you are better able to adapt and squash them quickly.

I agreed to attend paramedic school: a year-long commitment. It made college look like child's play. There were numerous medications I had to memorize, squiggly lines on a cardiac monitor were suddenly supposed to mean something and I had to practice intubations on real live people. All of this on top of family life with a wife and newborn kept me on my toes 24/7. But suddenly the things that triggered stressful emotions no longer did.

After getting my paramedic certification I felt like I could finally breathe again. I had so much more extra time which I had no idea what to do with. So, I did what any ordinary complacent person would,

I settled. I rode as a frontline medic for years. I aspired to be promoted to Sergeant, so I completed promotional testing. But that was it.

For three years straight I tested to be promoted. This promotional process included a written, driving and a physical test. After the completion of these you would get your scores tallied and would get to move on to the civil service interview if your scores were above the minimum threshold. The first two years I took the test I didn't even make it to the interview portion. I was embarrassed and beaten down. But just like my younger self, I didn't have self-confidence. I began to question if I should even keep testing for that position.

I told myself that I had studied and prepared as much as I could the past few years (that was a lie). What was the point if I wasn't even close? Then I finally realized the truth. I had turned complacent. I had been functioning as a front-line paramedic for

6 years and that's it. I wasn't investing in myself. I wasn't attending outside classes or trying to build on my knowledge. I had a piece of paper that said I could start IVs on people and that was good enough for me.

I had to channel that same energy I had back when I first started. When I was trying to invest in myself. For the next year I did nothing but build myself up like I was a business I had started and wanted to see succeed. I studied every chance I got, even on the toilet. Every shift I would go out and practice scenarios with our engine. I wrote pumping calculations on the white board at work like I was back in college math. I set up traffic cones and practiced driving every engine in our fleet.

I wanted this promotion, but I didn't even respect myself enough to build me up. How was I expected to be a leader to others if I couldn't showcase pure determination and grit to them?

The Salty Paramedic

The final written test I took before getting promoted had me more nervous than ever: 150 questions over multiple textbooks and I still thought I would fail despite reading them all multiple times. The proctor gave us all our booklets and informed us we would have 4 hours to take it. You would think someone that went over the study material as much as I did that year would have been more confident. I wasn't. I reluctantly turned my answers in and waited until everyone else was finished. When we reconvened and got our scores back, I looked down unimpressed. 85. It wasn't terrible, but I was really going to have to show out on the other parts of the testing to get the position I was seeking.

Driving was next. I pulled up to the course and saw the engine that drove like a rolling turd, nice. Going over on time and hitting cones would affect your score so I knew my best bet would be to stay calm. I had practiced this a million times, now I just had to do it again in front of a bunch of proctors. No big deal. I drove the course quickly but carefully and saw one total cone I hit out of my side view mirror. Even though I didn't receive my score right there I had a good feeling I did decent enough to stay in the game. The physical assessment was next.

People often joke about bubble guts while being nervous, but I think I had to go to the bathroom 3 times prior to taking the physical assessment. I showed up when my name was called and completed all the trials to the best of my ability. Now all that was left was to wait for an email saying I had received enough points to continue to the final interview.

After what seemed like an eternity, I received an email stating I was eligible to attend the interview. I instantly felt an immense weight lifted off my shoulders knowing I was still in the game. I watched multiple videos the weeks following of practice civil service questions and practiced my answers to family members. I had devoted hours of time preparing for this moment the year leading up to this. If I didn't get promoted, it only meant there were more qualified applicants because I knew I invested in myself this time and did everything I could.

I showed up to the interview in my Class A uniform with a fresh fade (they didn't give bonus points to a sweet haircut). I sat across from four people who proceeded to ask me questions about why I wanted the position and what I had done to prepare for it. I answered everything openly and honestly and walked out of the interview knowing no matter what happened, I had given it my all.

About a week later an email came across my phone. It was the promotional list. I quickly opened it and looked at the long list of names. To my astonishment, I was shown as #1. I had done it, after years of futile attempts I was going to get promoted.

After my promotion, I made it my mission to invest in myself. I never wanted to be stagnant again in my career. No matter where you are at currently there is always something you can do to improve yourself. Gaining knowledge is tremendously paramount in our job field. We owe it to ourselves, our families, our coworkers and the citizens we represent to build ourselves up into the most knowledgeable and efficient first responder we can be. It is entirely in our hands to improve as a person. The only reason you aren't improving is yourself.

I challenge you to list out all your goals on the next page that you want to accomplish over the next year, so that you can invest in yourself.

CHAPTER SIX

CREATE AN OUTLET

Individuals that make the job their whole personality really piss me off. That's rich coming from a guy that makes videos about the job on social media, right? It's not exactly what I mean, so let me explain my thinking to you.

We all know someone in our department or agency that eats, sleeps and breathes public service. Most people wouldn't think that's a bad thing, but it is. As I've touched on multiple times throughout this book, our careers bring stress daily. Individuals that perform the job, work constant overtime at the same job and then go home and think about the job are opening themselves up to destruction from the inside.

I truly believe we all need to have an outlet within our lives to channel out all the bad things we experience. This outlet can take many forms. If you go to your local fire department, I will challenge you not to find someone who has a part time job doing something they truly love. A lot of us do woodworking, landscaping or automobile work to name a few. Not only does this give us an extra income in a career field that typically doesn't offer enough to live, but it lets us have an outlet to decompress doing what we enjoy doing.

Now don't get your panties in a bunch, I know all of us don't need to have a second job. That's where you can have other kinds of outlets. Golf trip with the boys? That pretty much guarantees I will go back to work refreshed the shift after and not be thinking about anything that would trigger those job stressors. Do you like reading (other stuff than this shitty book)? Do you like to go hunting? There is a multitude of things we can do on our days off that will transform our worrisome mind and get a nice dopamine rush.

A year ago, I was the guy that ate, slept and breathed work. I worked a lot of overtime and didn't really have a hobby. I didn't have any good skills to create a side business so I kind of just became a cog in the machine. When my daughter was born, I was off work for six weeks for paternity leave, so I had more spare time than I knew what to do with.

Throughout my career, I was always the guy that would get texted to make a meme about a certain situation or edit someone's head on someone else's body to make light of something that happened at work. While I was sitting in the hospital with my wife and newborn daughter, I developed a wild hair to create a social media account and start posting my memes about the job for everyone to see.

Within a month I had thousands of people following and commenting on how much they appreciated the videos I was making. It was extremely weird for me that the stupid ideas in my head were developing into something where I could bring humor and laughter to people that worked the same job I did but lived halfway across the globe.

After a few months I had started to get approached by companies to do collaboration projects with them, magazine interviews and I even had content creators I had followed for years commenting on my stuff. What had started out as a joke had developed into a calling that I feel I will continue until I'm old and grey.

Still working as a firefighter/paramedic and content creator at the same time, I was able to start supplementing video work for a lot of the overtime hours. I was home more, and in turn around my wife and children more. It was night and day. A lot of the stress I harbored from being at work all the time was melting off. Although it might have seemed a stupid "side job" to most, I started to receive messages from people in my inbox that my content was helping their mental health after bad calls at work. These kind of messages to this day make everything I do regarding content creation completely worth it.

Creating an outlet, I believe, is super crucial to maintaining good mental health. If you do not currently have one, don't give up hope. There is something in this world that will give you happiness and a way for your mind to venture outside the bad parts of the job. You just need to find it.

I challenge you to write down on the next page what you enjoy doing (it could be multiple things). If you have free time, make sure to take time for yourself and enjoy these things in your life.

CHAPTER SEVEN

PRIORITIZE YOUR LIFE

Why do first responders want to take care of everyone but themselves? It's a question that has plagued generations. It's in our nature. We love the gratification of fixing someone else's problems, but we are often hard pressed to fix our own. Our priorities are organized from least important to most important, but the order you have them in is not good for your well-being at the end of the day.

Unfortunately, I believe most divorces among first responders can be contributed to either: infidelity or bad prioritizing. I'm not going to preach on infidelity, I'm no marriage counselor. That's for you and your spouse to work out. Prioritizing your life is something I love to speak strongly about, however.

This play considers a bunch of the others I have previously talked about in this book. Having your outlet? Yes, it's a great thing you need to have. But if it takes up all your time away from your family? No bueno.

Most of you reading this book work long hours. 12, 24 or even 48-hour shifts are the norm for you. We come home sleep-deprived and emotionally drained and are expected to be present for our family and to be the same type of individual you were when you saw them last. You can't be present? I don't want to hear that; this is what you signed up for.

As I touched on earlier, when I was a kid, my dad worked a ton of jobs. I remember my mom used to take me and my sister to the firehouse almost on a nightly basis just so we could get some time to see him. The number of hours he worked weekly was insane, but he maintained a healthy marriage and an even healthier relationship with his children. How did he do it? He prioritized his life.

My father had a few outlets. He would go golfing with his buddies. Have them over for poker night. He still took the time for himself when he needed to. But he didn't spend every free moment he had for himself. He delegated his time wisely. The times I do remember when my dad was home, it was fun every minute.

When it snowed, he would always make it his mission to take us to the biggest hill he could find to go sledding. If there was a school function or a sports game going on for me or my sister, he would make every possible effort to be there even if he had to show up in his duty uniform and on a fire truck. I would always remember him bringing my mom flowers for their anniversary or finding a babysitter so he could take her out to dinner.

Too many times during my life have I seen people in our field get divorced or get shunned by their kids. We let this career consume us and we often become blind to the people that need our care and attention the most.

As I got older, it was easy for me. I simply had to model what I saw growing up to properly allot the proper amount of time needed to take care of my wife, family and even myself. But not everyone has that guidance that I am still beyond thankful I received.

Unfortunately, I have seen too many people become selfish in their home life when they act selfless in their work life. Grown men and women that let their own egocentric desires take precedence over the individuals that depend on them.

Prioritizing yourself is important during certain times of your life, not constantly. That might sound contradictory to my whole mental health narrative, but if you properly take care of your family, then you will reap the benefits tenfold as opposed to if you just take care of yourself. If you show your family and friends the same care and devotion you give to your patients, your life has no choice but to be undeniably energetic and vibrant.

In summary, one must prioritize one's life to maintain mental health. You must always take the time to look after yourself no matter how hectic your life is. Also, one must find the correct balance in prioritization for every aspect of their life: friends, family and work. Some are more important than others and it's up to you to adequately address all of them appropriately.

Challenge yourself to write ways to prioritize your life on the following page. If you've got kids, think of a weekly event you all could do together no matter how small. Something they could look forward to. Maybe something you could do with your spouse weekly. Correct delegation of your time can keep your mental well-being in check.

Don't Lose Yourself

_____
_____
_____
_____
_____
_____
_____
_____
_____
_____
_____
_____
_____
_____
_____
_____
_____
_____
_____
_____
_____
_____

CHAPTER EIGHT

LAUGH

One of the phrases I heard the most growing up was "laughter is the best medicine." I truly believe that humor in this field will cure the majority of what you're feeling. That's part of the reason I continue to do my videos about the job online.

There are a few different types of humor: light-hearted and dark. Light-hearted could be the knock-knock joke that your five-year-old comes home and tells you after school or someone farting in the middle of an elevator. Dark humor is the type of thing we say back and forth to each other at the station after seeing some traumatic shit. The type of stuff that if a lay person heard would be up in arms to lock us all up. It's insane the type of stuff that can help us cope with trauma. I never understood it until I was in the job myself.

Growing up I was blessed to have a woman in my life that taught me how vital humor is in life. My grandmother watched me while I was growing up while my parents were at work. She was a strong-willed woman with a prosthetic leg that wouldn't think twice to threaten you to say she would hit you with it. She had been through more hardships than anyone I had known but still proceeded to smile about it and make people laugh.

Most of my childhood memories stemmed from her because they were just so damn funny. She would tell me to lay with her on the couch so she could tell me a story and then fart in my face, thinking it was hysterical even when I was gasping for air. She told me once to look in a bird feeder at a baby bird and waited until I was staring directly into the hole to smack the hell out of it and run away laughing. I quickly found out it was a not a baby bird, but a hornet's nest inside and I was quickly swarmed by the angry hornets.

Through all these crazy experiences it became very easy for me to learn to take a joke and perform them myself. April Fools Day quickly became my favorite holiday (it was hers as well) because I got to try to pull off crazier pranks than she did.

My grandmother kept the same fire throughout her whole life. She was a small-town legend. Everyone knew her because she was a stranger to no one and would always try to make you laugh. Her health had deteriorated almost overnight a few years ago and she ended up in the hospital. I still remember the hospital visits, where despite having very little to no energy, she would try to crack a joke with the nurse or a family member visiting. It was wild to me. She was in so much pain, so much mental anguish, but she was trying to laugh about it. She knew what had helped her endure the hardships in her life. Laughing had always been the best medicine.

When she was discharged from the hospital to go to the nursing home, I was given the unique opportunity to take her in my ambulance via inter-facility transfer. We arrived at her hospital room, and I walked in and instantly knew she wasn't herself. She looked extremely tired and weak. I knelt and whispered in her ear, "You ready to get out of here gran?" She mumbled something and mustered half a smile. We loaded her into the back of the ambulance, and I sat down next to my grandmother while we took her to the nursing home. After I got her hooked up to my cardiac monitor and got a baseline set of vitals, I sat down to hopefully have a conversation with her. A conversation with that wonderful lady that helped raise me. She wasn't there anymore. Her eyes were glassy, and she had a blank stare. I tried talking to her but the most I got out of her was a few smiles here or there. When we arrived at the nursing home, I helped transfer her over to her bed and put a warm blanket on her. I kneeled and kissed her and went back to the station. That ride back was rough. My mind was running a mile a minute. I had witnessed death tons of times in my life, but I knew this one was going to hit me hard. One of the brightest lights in my life was about to burn out and I knew it.

A few days after this she was sent back to the hospital. My wife and I were lucky enough to make it there in time and tell her we were pregnant. She smiled, and then a few hours after we had left, I received a call that she had passed. On April Fools Day too, of all days.

That same woman that had taught multiple generations of a family and a community that laughing was ok, was no longer here. I prepared a speech at her funeral because I felt like I owed her that much. I spoke about the impact her humor had on my life and how I conducted myself in my career. Kind of like I'm detailing in this book. I owed this woman the world, because I believe she has helped save my sanity more than a handful of times. Never underestimate the power of humor, it has more of an impact than you realize.

As I've navigated my career, I've become accustomed to meeting individuals that are the no-bullshit type. They don't like to laugh or have fun. Strictly business. That's all well and good if you're the CEO of a multi-million-dollar corporation. But we work in public service. We witness the shit of nightmares. And you know what helps quell nightmares? Laugh right in the face of the demons staring back at you.

On the next page, I challenge you to write a few of the best station pranks or jokes you have witnessed. Hold onto these memories. Laughter can illuminate a dark room.

AFTERWORD

This book had been embedded in my mind for the last few years, but I had always been unsure how to put the right words onto paper. Throughout my life I have witnessed suicides, mental breakdowns, panic attacks and depression. If this book has helped save one single person, then it has accomplished its intended purpose. I made it my mission to try to help first responders through my videos, and now this book, cope with the type of things they see. If you are struggling, please utilize the resources included on the following page.

Don't Lose Yourself.

-The Salty Paramedic

National Suicide Prevention Lifeline

1-800-273-8255

Copline (Law Enforcement Only)

1-800-267-5463

Frontline Helpline

 1-866-676-7500

Safe Call Now (staffed by first responders)

1-206-459-3020 or 1-877-230-6060

Made in the USA
Monee, IL
23 March 2025

14447555R00049